FORENSIC SCIENCE INVESTIGATED

FAMOUS | FORENSIC CASES

WRITTEN BY:
Rebecca Stefoff

mc Marshall Cavendish
Benchmark
New York

MARSHALL CAVENDISH BENCHMARK
99 WHITE PLAINS ROAD
TARRYTOWN, NEW YORK 10591-9001
www.marshallcavendish.us

LIBRARY OF CONGRESS CATALOGING-IN-PUBLICATION DATA
Stefoff, Rebecca, 1951-
Famous forensic cases / by Rebecca Stefoff.
p. cm. — (Forensic science investigated)
Includes bibliographical references and index.
ISBN 978-0-7614-3082-7
1. Forensic sciences—Case studies—Juvenile literature. I. Title.
HV8073.S7314 2009
363.25—dc22
2008003634

EDITOR: Christina Gardeski   PUBLISHER: Michelle Bisson
ART DIRECTOR: Anahid Hamparian   SERIES DESIGNER: Kristen Branch

Photo Research by Anne Burns Images

Cover Photo by *Corbis*/Tetra Images Back Cover Photo by *Phototake*/Terry Why

The photographs in this book are used with permission and through the courtesy of:
iStockphoto: pp. 1, 3 (hand Chris Hutchinson, cells David Marchal). *The Halifax Herald
Limited*: pp. 4, 71. *Corbis*: p. 6 Alissa Crandall; pp. 15, 16 Bettman; p. 19 Hulton Deutsch
Collection; p. 33 Yves Forestier/Sygma; p. 40 Vienna Report Agency/Sygma. *The
Associated Press*: pp. 12, 20, 23, 25, 37, 44, 54, 65, 76, 82. *Alamy Images*: p. 30 MShields
Photos; p. 56 ImageState; p. 59 David Wall; p. 61 Ern Mainka; p. 79 Images of Africa
Photobank. *The Innocence Project*: p. 75.

Printed in Malaysia
1 3 5 6 4 2

Cover: The goal of forensic science is to serve justice by finding the truth.

CONTENTS

Clayton Johnson claimed he had not murdered his wife. Forensic investigators would recreate the scene of her death to test his claim.

WHAT IS FORENSICS?

A WOMAN LIES AT the bottom of a staircase, bleeding from a fatal head wound. Did she fall, or did someone strike her on the head? A jury finds her husband guilty of murder and sentences him to life in prison. He swears he is innocent, but can he prove it?

The beaches of western Alaska are a gruesome sight. The bodies of several hundred walruses have washed up onto the shore, and the huge marine mammals—protected by law—are missing their heads. Were they illegally killed for their ivory tusks?

A serial killer murders women on two continents. Police are sure that they know the killer's identity, but

▲ The walrus's ivory tusks make this marine mammal a target for illegal hunters. Such cases make gruesome work for wildlife forensic specialists.

they need solid evidence. All they can find is a single stray hair. Will it be enough?

Forensic science, which is the use of scientific methods and tools to investigate crimes and bring suspects to trial, helped solve each of these cases. The term "forensic" comes from ancient Rome, where people debated matters of law in a public meeting place called the Forum. The Latin word *forum* gave rise to *forensic,* meaning "relating to courts of law or to public debate."

Today "**forensics**" has several meanings. One is the art of speaking in debates, which is why some schools have forensics clubs or teams for students who want to learn debating skills. The best-known meaning of "forensics," though, is crime solving through forensic science.

Fascination with forensics explains the popularity of many recent TV shows, movies, and books, but crime and science have been linked for a long time. The first science used in criminal investigation was medicine, and one of the earliest reports of forensic medicine comes from ancient Rome. In 44 BCE, the Roman leader Julius Caesar was stabbed to death not far from the Forum. A physician named Antistius examined the body and found that Caesar had received twenty-three stab wounds, but only one wound was fatal. Antistius had performed one of history's first recorded postmortem examinations, in which a physician looks at a body to find out how the person died. But forensics has always had limits. Antistius could point out the chest wound that had killed Caesar, but he could not say who had struck the deadly blow.

Death in its many forms inspired the first forensic manuals. The oldest one was published in China in 1248. Called *Hsi duan yu* (The Washing Away of Wrongs), it tells how the bodies of people who have been strangled differ from those of drowning victims. When a corpse is recovered from the water, says the manual, officers of the law should examine the tissues and small bones in the neck. Torn tissues and broken bones show that the victim met with foul play before being thrown into the water.

Poison became another landmark in the history of forensics in 1813, when Mathieu Orfila, a professor of medical and forensic chemistry at the University of Paris, published *Traité des poisons* (A Treatise on Poisons). Orfila described the deadly effects of various mineral, vegetable, and animal substances. He laid the foundation of the modern science of **toxicology**, the branch of forensics that deals with poisons, drugs, and their effects on the human body.

As France's most famous expert on poisons, Orfila played a part in an 1840 criminal trial that received wide publicity. Marie LaFarge was accused of murder after the death of her husband. Orfila testified that he had examined the man's corpse and found traces of arsenic. LaFarge said that she had not fed the arsenic to her husband and insisted that he must have eaten it while away from home. The court, however, sentenced her to life imprisonment. Pardoned in 1850 after ten years in prison, LaFarge died the next year, claiming innocence to the end.

Cases such as the LaFarge trial highlighted the growing use of medical evidence in criminal investigations and trials. Courts were recognizing other kinds of forensic evidence, too. As early as 1784 a British murder case had been decided by physical evidence. The torn edge of a piece of newspaper found in the pocket of a suspect named John Toms matched the torn edge of a ball of paper found in the wound of a man who had been killed by a pistol shot to the head (at the time people used rolled pieces of cloth or paper, called wadding, to hold bullets firmly in gun barrels). Because the paper was a clear link to the deadly shot, Toms was declared guilty of murder. Fifty-one years later, an officer of Scotland Yard, Britain's famous police division, caught a murderer by using a flaw on the fatal bullet to trace the bullet to its maker. Such cases marked the birth of ballistics, the branch of forensics that deals with firearms.

Not all forensic developments involved murder. Science also helped solve crimes such as arson and forgery. By the early nineteenth century, chemists had developed the first tests to identify certain dyes used in ink. Experts could then determine the age and chemical makeup of the ink on documents that were suspected of being fakes, such as wills and valuable manuscripts.

Forensics started to become a regular part of police work at the end of the nineteenth century, after an Austrian law professor named Hans Gross published a two-volume handbook on the subject in 1893. Gross's book, usually referred to as *Criminal Investigation*, brought together all the many techniques that scientists and law enforcers had developed for examining the physical evidence of crime—bloodstains, bullets, and more. Police departments started using *Criminal Investigation* to train officers. The book entered law school courses as well.

Modern forensic experts regard Hans Gross as the founder of their profession. Among other contributions, Gross invented the word "criminalistics" to refer to the general study of crime or criminals. Today, however, the term has a narrower, more specific meaning. It refers to the study of physical evidence from crime scenes.

Almost every branch of science has been involved in criminal investigations. Meteorologists have testified about the weather on the date of a crime. Botanists have named the plants that produced tiny specks of pollen found on suspects' clothes. Dentists have matched bite marks on victims' bodies to the teeth of their killers. Wildlife biologists have investigated cases of illegal hunting and trade in endangered species.

Criminalistics—the collecting, protecting, and examining of crime scene evidence—is the basis for these and other forms of forensic investigation. Whether they are called criminalists, crime scene investigators (CSIs), or scene-of-crime officers (SOCOs), the men and women who collect the physical and biological signs of crime are the first to give the evidence a chance to speak—to reveal what really happened. Scientists who work in crime labs, universities, and private companies around the world perform tests on forensic evidence or serve as expert witnesses to interpret it in courtrooms. By bringing the evidence to life, forensic specialists help law enforcement agencies solve crimes, playing a key role in dramas of life and death.

Sir Bernard Spilsbury, a witness in some of Britain's most notorious murder cases, was a forensic scientist who became as famous as any celebrity.

CHAPTER ONE

THE FIRST FORENSICS SUPERSTAR

▼ **FOR MORE THAN THIRTY YEARS,**
from 1910 until the mid–1940s, the best-known forensic scientist in England was Sir Bernard Spilsbury. He brought medical training and a sharp, logical mind to bear on hundreds of criminal investigations. Spilsbury was a **pathologist**, a doctor who examines corpses to determine the cause of death, but he was knowledgeable about other branches of forensics as well.

Spilsbury examined hundreds of crime scenes, performed more than 25,000 **autopsies**, and testified as an expert witness in many trials. On the witness stand he was calm and dignified, always able to explain scientific matters clearly and with an air of authority. His manner made a profound and convincing impression on juries, which were beginning to develop an interest in forensics.

Colin Evans, author of a number of books about the history of forensic science, has called Spilsbury the "father of forensics." In Spilsbury's day, forensics was just becoming an important part of crime investigation. Spilsbury came to be regarded as a celebrity whose investigations were eagerly reported by the press. He was one of the first forensic specialists who was well known to the public.

▶ THE BODY IN THE BASEMENT

Spilsbury was involved in some of the most notorious cases of his time. In 1910 he helped examine the badly decomposed remains of a dismembered body that had been found buried in the cellar of a London house. The house was occupied by an American named Hawley Harvey Crippen, whose wife, Cora, had been missing for months. After Cora's disappearance, Crippen had begun a love affair with a young woman. When people started asking questions about Crippen's missing wife, he fled with the young woman to Belgium and then to Canada, where they were arrested. Crippen reportedly told the officer who arrested him that he was glad to have been caught.

▲ Police officers escort the accused murderer Crippen, his face muffled by a scarf, from the ship on which he had fled to Canada after his wife's disappearance.

Meanwhile, several pathologists examined the grisly remains from the basement. The head was missing, and there were no bones, just pieces of tissue and organs. Among them was a piece of skin with a horseshoe-shaped scar. Spilsbury, whose career was just getting started, had made a special study of scars. He identified the scar on the skin from Crippen's home as the type that would result from a hysterectomy, an operation that Cora was known to have had.

▲ Crippen and Ethel Le Neve, his girlfriend, stand trial for the murder of Crippen's wife. The jury would find Le Neve not guilty.

In a dramatic demonstration, Spilsbury brought his microscope and the skin fragment to the court so that the jurors could see the evidence for themselves as he explained its significance. His expert testimony convinced the jury that the remains were those of Crippen's wife.

The jury believed that the remains from the cellar were those of Cora Crippen, but did that mean that her husband had murdered her? If she had died by accident—such as an accidental overdose of drugs—

Crippen might have concealed the body in a fit of panic, fearing that he would be accused of murder. The brutal way in which the body had been mutilated and hidden, however, led most observers to think the worst. Crippen was found guilty and hanged for Cora's murder, protesting to the end that he had not killed his wife.

▶ BRIDES AND BATHTUBS

A few years after the Crippen case, Spilsbury solved the crime that came to be known as the "brides in the bath." George Joseph Smith had been married three times. Each wife died not long after the marriage. Smith benefited from their deaths, receiving money from life insurance or wills.

All three women died in exactly the same way— accidental drowning in the bathtub of a rented house or apartment. Investigators at Scotland Yard, Britain's famous police division, did not think this series of deaths was simply a tragic coincidence. They suspected that Smith had murdered his wives, but there were no marks of violence on the women's bodies, no traces of poison in their systems. No one could figure out how Smith could have drowned three women in shallow water without any sign of struggle or disturbance. Two of the women were tall, strong, and vigorous. Why hadn't they fought back?

THE CRIPPEN CASE, complete with a scandalous love affair as well as ghastly details about the mutilated body, was one of the most sensational newspaper stories ever to grip Britain. For more than a century it had a prominent place in true-crime books. Then, in 2007, the case took a surprising twist, thanks to modern crime-solving technology.

Forensic experts in Michigan (Crippen's home state) got hold of the very same microscope slide that Spilsbury had used in court to show the victim's abdominal tissue to the jurors. The slide had been preserved in the Royal London Hospital Archives and Museum. The investigators obtained DNA from the tissue sample, then compared it with DNA from three living women believed to be descended from Cora Crippen's mother. These three women share the same mitochondrial DNA (mtDNA), a type of DNA that passes from one generation to the next by way of the females in a family. Cora Crippen and the other descendants of her mother would have inherited the same mtDNA. The mtDNA from Spilsbury's tissue sample, however, was different from that of the living women.

Some forensic experts have questioned the results of the test. The chemical preservatives used on the tissue sample from the Crippen trial could have contaminated the DNA, for example, making the test unreliable. Or perhaps the living women were not really descended from Cora

WAS CRIPPEN A KILLER, OR WAS HE SIMPLY HORRIBLY UNLUCKY? MODERN FORENSIC SCIENCE HAS CAST A SHADOW OF DOUBT OVER THE CASE THAT HAS FASCINATED CRIMINOLOGISTS SINCE 1910.

Crippen's mother. But the Michigan investigators think that the results are clear: The grisly finds in that London basement could not be the remains of Cora Crippen. If they are right, who was the victim? Who dismembered a woman's body, leaving traces in the cellar? And what happened to Cora Crippen? Spilsbury may have correctly identified the hysterectomy scar—but no one considered the possibility that the remains in Crippen's cellar were not those of Cora Crippen. The case, it appears, may not be closed after all.

· · · · ·

▲ This picture probably celebrated Beatrice "Bessie" Mundy's marriage to a man she knew as Henry Williams. In reality, he was George Joseph Smith, who would soon be charged with her murder.

After reviewing the medical literature on drowning and examining the fatal bathtubs, Spilsbury came up with a theory about how Smith could have committed the murders. In certain rare cases, people have died after jumping feet-first into water—not by drowning, but because the sudden rush of water into the nose had affected the vagus nerve, which runs from the brain to the center of the body. Physicians use the term "vagal inhibition" to describe a sudden shock or pressure to that nerve. Vagal inhibition causes instant unconsciousness, followed swiftly by death because the nerve sends a message to the brain that causes the heart to stop beating. The medical books Spilsbury read told how vagal inhibition had killed people who had jumped into water, but he realized that it was the force of water striking the nerve in the back of the nose, not the act of jumping, that had brought death.

Spilsbury showed how Smith could have killed each wife by approaching her while she was taking a bath, then swiftly and suddenly jerking her feet or knees high into the air. This would have pulled her head forcefully under water, causing water to rush into her nose. Vagal inhibition would make her lose consciousness and die, but she would look like a victim of accidental drowning. During Smith's trial Spilsbury brought one of the fatal bathtubs into the courtroom, along with a diagram showing how the murder could have been committed. The jury found Smith guilty. Like Crippen, he was hanged.

▶ UP IN SMOKE

Spilsbury was occasionally baffled over the course of his career, and he made some mistakes, but for the most part he was able to make sense of the often gruesome evidence he examined. One of his biggest challenges was the 1930 case that the newspapers called "the body in the blazing car."

An hour or so after midnight on November 6, 1930, two young men named Alfred Brown and William Bailey were walking home from a dance in a rural area near the English town of Northampton when they saw a fire ahead of them. At first they thought nothing of it, because in England November 5 is Guy Fawkes Day, a holiday traditionally celebrated with bonfires. As Brown and Bailey approached the fire, a man suddenly appeared on the road. He seemed startled to see them, and after a few mumbled words about a holiday bonfire he hurried away. When Brown and Bailey approached the fire, however, they saw that it was no ordinary Guy Fawkes bonfire: it was an automobile on the side of the road, engulfed in flames. They ran to the nearest village to get the police.

▲ The burned car beside this rural road held crucial evidence in one of the most perplexing cases of Spilsbury's career.

The blazing car, it turned out, contained a body that was burned beyond recognition. Much of the car was badly burned, too, but amazingly, the license plate remained. Using the plate, police traced the car to its owner, Alfred Rouse, who lived in a London suburb. When the London police went to Rouse's home, his wife, Lily, told them that her husband was a traveling salesman. He was away on business. Rouse was indeed away from home, but not on business. He was in a tiny village in Wales, the home of a girlfriend named Ivy Jenkins. He had arrived there by bus because, as he told Ivy, his car had been stolen.

Meanwhile, the crime scene was being badly mishandled. Local police constables had moved the car away from the road because they feared it would block traffic. Unfortunately, they had neglected to take photographs of its original position. In fact, they had not even made notes. Then, when they removed the charred corpse from the wreck—again without pictures or notes of its position—they had left the crime scene unguarded. Newspaper photographers arrived and, to create more dramatic images, began rearranging pieces of evidence, such as a radiator cap and other pieces of auto equipment that had been scattered around. The idea that a crime scene should be left untouched until the arrival of skilled investigators had not yet filtered through to rural police departments.

Rouse was horrified when the discovery of his burned-out car, containing a corpse, appeared on the front page of the newspaper. He told Ivy and her family that something horrible must have happened after his car had been stolen, and said that he would travel by bus to London to clear up the matter. An acquaintance in Wales, suspicious of Rouse's story, telephoned Scotland Yard. When Rouse's bus reached London, a detective boarded and took Rouse into custody. Immediately Rouse began talking.

The stolen-car story, he admitted, was a lie. What had really happened was that he had picked up a hitchhiker.

Rouse later stopped the car and asked the hitchhiker to fill the gas tank from a can of gasoline sitting on the backseat. Rouse was several yards away from the car when he saw it burst into flame. Realizing that there was nothing he could do to save the hitchhiker, he fled in panic. The fire, he said, must have started through some terrible accident involving a fuel leak.

▲ Alfred Rouse's scandalous secret life turned the public—and the jury—against him.

The police might have accepted Rouse's version of events except that Rouse, like many criminals before and after him, did not know when to stop talking. He boasted to the police officers about his relationships with many women, whom he called his "harem," and complained that keeping up so many relationships was expensive. This made police dig into Rouse's private life. What they discovered made headlines across Britain and shocked the readers who devoured the press accounts of the case.

In addition to being a bigamist—someone illegally married to two spouses at the same time—Rouse also had long-standing relationships with several other women. He was supporting a number of children by these lovers, and he was deeply in debt. The police now looked at the case of the blazing car in a different light. Had Rouse tried to stage his own disappearance to escape his burden of debt and tangled relationships? If so, Rouse might have murdered the man in the car, hoping that the body would be mistaken for his own, then lost his nerve and fled to Ivy's home, where he was known by his real name.

▶ SPILSBURY SPEAKS

Northampton law enforcement authorities had wanted to control the investigation of the Rouse case, and a local pathologist had performed a preliminary autopsy on the burned body. Four days after the fire, however, Scotland Yard sent Sir Bernard Spilsbury to Northampton. The famous forensic pathologist faced a very difficult job. The evidence had been manhandled, and he could not know for sure what the crime scene had originally looked like. The body had been partly dissected in the earlier autopsy, so Spilsbury also had to deal with a secondhand set of remains. Still, he made some important findings.

Spilsbury's primary concern was identifying the body, but he soon realized that would be impossible.

The lower parts of both arms and both legs had been completely destroyed by the fire. The face and ears were gone, and the skull had split from the heat. The body was so badly burned that its gender was uncertain—the first pathologist had originally thought it was a woman, then decided that it was a man. After finding a fragment of burned trousers attached to the body, Spilsbury also concluded that the victim was male, and Rouse's confession soon supported this opinion.

Spilsbury also looked at the victim's teeth. They seemed to be those of a person in his twenties. Signs of decay and neglect suggested that the victim had not been able to afford dental care. The victim's lungs were stained black on the inside, a condition that Spilsbury had seen in men who worked in coal mines. Rouse claimed he had not asked his passenger's name, and in spite of a wide-ranging investigation and large rewards offered by the newspapers, the burned man was never identified.

The stranger's identity remained a mystery, but his cause of death was clear. Soot in the throat and internal organs colored bright pink (a sign of carbon monoxide poisoning) indicated that the man had died of fire-related shock within 30 seconds of first inhaling smoke from the fire. But a vital question remained: Why didn't the victim get out of the car? The body had been found facedown on the front seat, yet the fire had started in the rear of the car. There should have been time for the man to escape. Rouse's story was so suspicious that he was charged with murder. The police thought that their suspect had knocked the victim out and then set fire to him and the automobile.

Rouse had claimed that his passenger must have started the fire by lighting a cigar while filling the gas tank, but the position of the man's body made that claim ridiculous. Everyone who had seen the corpse in the car before it was moved agreed that one leg had been stretched out straight. As the man lay on the car seat, his leg must have been sticking out through the open door.

Spilsbury was the key witness for the prosecution. His testimony made it clear that although fire can make muscles contract, doubling up a body, it cannot make them extend or stretch a limb. The only explanation for the position of the burned corpse was that the door was open when the fire started, and the victim was lying on the seat with one leg sticking out. Spilsbury also testified that the fire had very quickly reached temperatures hot enough to melt the car's brass fixtures. This could happen only if gasoline had been present both in the passenger compartment and under the car, where the fire had started.

Rouse took the witness stand in his own defense, but he did more harm than good. He acted cocky and clever, and he showed no remorse that an unknown man had perished in his car. "It is very unfortunate, that is all I can say," was his only comment about the death. Rouse's attitude on the witness stand, together with the scandalous revelations about his personal life, turned the jury against him. Yet Spilsbury's testimony about the significance of the position of the corpse in the burned-out car carried the most influence with the jurors. The only explanation, they felt, was that Rouse had set an unconscious man on fire. They convicted him of murder.

Shortly before his execution, Rouse wrote a confession in which he admitted his guilt. He had met the victim a few days before the fire and decided that he would be a good "substitute" for himself in a faked accidental death. The man wanted a ride from one part of the country to another, so Rouse arranged to pick him up on Guy Fawkes night. Rouse supplied his passenger with whiskey to make him drowsy. When the man fell into a doze, Rouse stopped the car and strangled him until he lost consciousness. Rouse then poured gasoline over the motionless man, loosened part of the fuel system so that more gas would pour out under the car, and then set the victim and car afire. In spite of the sloppy treatment of the crime scene by local authorities, Sir Bernard Spilsbury's reconstruction of the crime had been accurate.

A laboratory technician removes a DNA sample from a micro test tube. Since the 1980s, DNA has become one of the most useful tools in forensic science.

CHAPTER TWO

CATCHING KILLERS WITH
SCIENCE

shrieks out," wrote an English playwright named John Webster in 1623. Murder has long been recognized as one of the worst crimes. Modern law enforcement agencies, such as police departments and the Federal Bureau of Investigation (FBI), generally give priority to cases of homicide. Although forensic science applies to all kinds of investigations, many new forensic tools and techniques have seen their first use in solving real-life murder mysteries.

▶ STALKING A SERIAL KILLER

In 1990 a young woman named Blanka Bockova was found dead in a wooded area of Prague, capital of the Czech Republic in central Europe. She had been strangled with her stockings, which were knotted together. Law enforcement investigators learned that she had been seen talking with a well-dressed stranger shortly before her death, but no one could identify the stranger, and police had not gathered any useful clues from the body or the crime scene. The case remained unsolved, but it was filed with the International Criminal Police Organization. Better known as Interpol, this organization coordinates investigations among law enforcement agencies in more than 180 countries.

The following year, police in the neighboring country of Austria investigated a string of unsolved murders of prostitutes who had been strangled with their pantyhose, then dumped in remote wooded locations. Although Austrian law enforcement authorities decided the cases were not the work of the same killer, the press was convinced that a single murderer was responsible. The papers declared that a serial killer was on the loose. When a retired police detective named August Schenner stepped forward to tell his story, the Austrian authorities realized that the press might be right.

News accounts of the murders had reminded Schenner of an investigation he had led in 1973. The

▲ Founded in Austria in 1923, the international police organization called Interpol has operated out of this headquarters in Lyons, France, since 1989.

victim, a prostitute, had been strangled with her stockings and thrown into a lake. Schenner's investigation had convinced him that the killer was a young man named Johann "Jack" Unterweger. By the time Schenner had built his case, however, Unterweger was already standing trial for the murder of another woman who had been found dead in the woods, strangled with her bra. Convicted for that murder, Unterweger was sent to prison for life. A forensic psychologist who examined Unterweger at the time described him as "enormously aggressive" and "sadistic" and had predicted that he would certainly kill again.

Even though Schenner's case did not go to trial, the detective had never forgotten his dangerous suspect. Schenner was horrified to learn that Unterweger had been released after serving fifteen years of his sentence, just months before the murdered women started turning up in Austria. Unterweger had managed to get a parole hearing because he had become a literary celebrity. He had entered prison as the illiterate son of a prostitute, but there he taught himself to read and write, and he set out to become a successful author. In his cell he had turned out poems and plays. His 1984 autobiography *Fegefeur (Purgatory)* became a best seller and was made into a movie.

Unterweger claimed to be reformed, no longer filled with rage, and said that he wanted to help society. Admirers of his writing felt that he had been rehabilitated, or turned into a better person. They mounted a movement to get him a parole hearing. In 1990 they succeeded, and after the hearing Unterweger was released from prison. He immediately became part of the nightclub scene, and he also appeared on radio and television talk shows. When Austria's prostitute murders started, Unterweger wrote and talked about the cases. He interviewed prostitutes and badgered police to do something. Fans of his writing thought that his background gave him special insight into the subject. A literary magazine hired Unterweger to write about prostitution in Los Angeles.

After Schenner's tip, the Austrian police placed Unterweger under surveillance, but just a few days later, in June of 1991, the writer left for Los Angeles. No prostitutes were murdered in Austria while he was out of the country. Investigators now considered Unterweger a prime suspect in the murders.

In Los Angeles, however, three prostitutes were murdered in June and July of 1991. Their bodies were found in remote wooded regions. Each had been strangled with her own bra. The knots used to tie the bras, investigators would later discover, were unusual—and identical to those found in the pantyhose that had strangled the Austrian victims.

▶ A SINGLE STRAND OF PROOF

After Unterweger returned to Austria, several women went missing. By the time their bodies were found, the murderer-turned-writer was the subject of a huge police investigation. Police got hold of his credit card records, which showed that he had been in the same city as each murdered woman at the time she was killed. Yet this could have been coincidence. It was not proof. Red fibers had been found on one body, and police discovered a red scarf in Unterweger's apartment that seemed to match the fibers. The fibers were not proof, though, because they could have come from a similar scarf.

The Unterweger investigation caused an uproar in the Austrian media. Unterweger's supporters accused the police of hounding the author because of his past. Fearing that he was about to be arrested, Unterweger fled with a girlfriend to Miami. When the fugitives contacted the girl's mother and asked her to send them money, the older woman told Unterweger that she would do so. But when Unterweger went to pick up the money, U.S. officials were waiting. The girl's mother had alerted the authorities. Unterweger was arrested on the charge of entering the country illegally, because on his entry papers he had not admitted having a criminal record.

While Unterweger was being held on the immigration charge, investigators from Los Angeles interviewed him about the killings there. Warned that he could face the death penalty if convicted of murder in California,

▲ Jack Unterweger, a convicted murderer turned literary celebrity, is escorted from Florida to Austria to stand trial for more murders.

Unterweger agreed to be extradited, or sent back to Austria, to face charges there. He returned to his homeland in May 1992. While in jail awaiting trial, he wrote letters to the newspapers defending himself. He still had many supporters who believed in his innocence.

Serial murder was almost unknown in Austria in the early 1990s, so Austrian authorities turned to more experienced American investigators for help. Details of the Los Angeles and Austrian murders were fed into the FBI's Violent Criminal Apprehension Program (VICAP), a computerized system that analyzes and compares features of crimes and crime scenes. The results suggested that all the murders had very likely been committed by a single person. In addition, FBI profilers—experts in criminal behavior—found links between the behavior shown in those crimes and Unterweger's first murder, back in 1973. American crime lab experts also helped with a study of the deadly knots, proving that those in the American and Austrian murders were identical.

Authorities in Austria, however, knew that their case against Unterweger was based on circumstantial evidence. The evidence, in other words, said that Unterweger *could* have committed the crimes, but it did not say that he *did* commit them. To prosecute Unterweger, the authorities needed something stronger, such as physical evidence linking Unterweger with one or more of the murdered women. Searches of the suspect's clothes and apartment, however, had failed to turn up anything usable. Police had learned that Unterweger had owned six cars in less than two years, and they had tracked down and searched the cars he had owned at the times of the Austrian murders. They found nothing. There was one last chance. Unterweger's credit card records showed that he had visited Prague in 1990. A check of Interpol's records showed that Blanka Bockova was killed during Unterweger's stay in Prague. Details of that crime matched the VICAP pattern.

Investigators managed to locate the car Unterweger had owned at the time of his visit to Prague. Hoping that the car might still contain a trace of evidence after several years, they made a painstaking forensic search, vacuuming every surface. They located a single hair, which they sent to a laboratory in Switzerland to be tested for DNA. Although the amount of genetic material in the root of the hair was extremely small, the lab was able to test it. The result showed a high degree of certainty that the hair was Blanka Bockova's. There was just a single chance in 2.1 million that the hair could have come from someone else. The police had their proof.

By placing one of the victims in Jack Unterweger's car, that single hair brought the suspect's claim of innocence crashing down. He went to trial for eleven murders—one in Prague, three in Los Angeles, and seven in Austria—and was convicted of nine (two of

▲ Unterweger's murder trial created a media frenzy.
Supporters of the successful, charming ex-convict insisted
that he had reformed.

the Austrian bodies were too badly decomposed to
show the cause of death). Unterweger faced a life sentence without hope of another parole. He had vowed
that he would never go back to prison, and this time he
told the truth. He hanged himself in his cell, using the
same knot police had found on his victims.

The Unterweger case is a good example of international crime-solving cooperation. It also illustrates the
way in which different kinds of forensic evidence can
come together to reinforce other kinds of detective work.

Cracking the Unterweger case involved traditional detective methods, such as tracking a suspect's movements, and modern forensics, such as fiber and knot analysis, behavioral patterning, and above all, laboratory analysis of DNA samples. Using science to solve crimes can sometimes lead investigators in two different directions, however, as the case of Susan Jaeger shows.

▶ TWO DISAPPEARANCES

In June 1973 the Jaeger family of Michigan went on a camping trip in Montana. One night as they slept in their tent, someone crept up to the campsite and kidnapped seven-year-old Susan Jaeger. After the little girl had been missing for twenty-four hours, the case was turned over to federal authorities. The FBI sent agents to Bozeman, Montana, near the site of Susan's disappearance. At the same time, profilers Howard Teten and Pat Mullany at the FBI's Behavioral Sciences Unit (BSU) in Washington, D.C., studied the case.

A profiler starts by reviewing everything that is known about a crime. Then, based on the ever-growing body of knowledge about previous crimes and known criminals, the profiler creates a description, or profile, of the kind of person most likely to have committed the crime. Although the Jaeger kidnapping offered few real clues, Teten and Mullany came up with some general ideas. The kidnapper, they said, was probably young, white, and male. He lived in the area. He had stumbled across the family's campsite by chance, then acted on impulse. The two profilers regretfully told Pete Dunbar, the FBI special agent in charge of the case, that Susan probably would not be recovered alive.

Dunbar received an anonymous phone call that contained a tip. The caller suggested a local suspect: David Meierhofer, a twenty-three-year-old veteran of the Vietnam War. Although Meierhofer matched the profile prepared by Teten and Mullany, the same characteristics described many other young men as well. Dunbar interviewed Meierhofer and found him pleasant, intelligent, and cooperative. There was no evidence against him, so he was released. The Jaegers returned to Michigan, clinging to the hope that their daughter might yet be found.

In January 1974 friends reported that an 18-year-old Bozeman woman was missing. She had recently stopped seeing her boyfriend, who had been angry about the break-up. The boyfriend was David Meierhofer. Police interviewed Meierhofer again. This time he offered to take two tests, known informally as **truth serum** and the **lie detector**. Both are highly controversial within the fields of law enforcement and science.

▶ PENTOTHAL, POLYGRAPHS, AND PROFILES

So-called truth serum is sodium thiopental (also called thiopental sodium and, under a brand name, Pentothal). It is a drug that is used to make people unconscious for surgery. It has also been given to condemned prisoners before they are injected with lethal drugs. Smaller doses of sodium thiopental, however, can make people feel relaxed and talkative.

The nickname "truth serum" is misleading. The drug does not compel people to tell the truth. A person under the influence of sodium thiopental cannot be made to reveal anything. Some subjects, however, lose their train of thought and wind up revealing more than they had intended. Others control themselves better, sticking to a false story throughout their questioning. Although law enforcement agencies have used sodium thiopental to make suspects chatty and cooperative, the results are unreliable, and they are not admissible as evidence in court.

"Lie detector" is another misleading label. The instrument that is sometimes called a lie detector is actually a **polygraph**, and it cannot detect lies. Rather, it records certain kinds of physical changes, such as sudden perspiration or altered rates of breathing and heartbeat. The polygraph consists of various sensors attached to the subject's body and a system of recording

▲ A Philadelphia newspaper sponsored a 2002 polygraph test for city councilman Frank DiCicco, who claimed that another councilman had made an ethnic slur.

their readings. Polygraph readings used to appear as sets of lines drawn on rolls of paper by moving pens; today, digital polygraphs present the readings as computer data.

Supporters of polygraph testing claim that when someone lies, uncontrollable physical reactions take place. Many believe that by asking a series of questions and then examining the record of the subject's responses, a skilled polygraph examiner can tell the difference between truthful answers and lies.

Ever since polygraphs were introduced in the 1920s, however, critics have questioned their usefulness. The polygraph measures physical changes that are signs of stress, but the stress is not necessarily caused by lying. Some subjects show high levels of stress during polygraph tests even when they give truthful answers to innocent questions such as "Does two plus two equal four?" Even more troubling is the fact that interpreting the test results is by no means an exact science. Many experiments have shown that different polygraph operators, when shown the same list of questions and the same set of polygraph results, often interpret the results in opposite ways.

Doubts about the scientific worth of polygraph results led the U.S. Supreme Court to ban them as trial evidence in 1923, and no one can be forced to take a polygraph test as part of a criminal investigation. Today, many experts in psychology and biomedical instruments consider polygraphy to be "junk science," something that claims to be scientific but hasn't been scientifically proven. They also point out that there are many well-known ways for subjects to "beat the test"—to control their physical reactions in ways that make the reading worthless.

The polygraph has never been widely used outside the United States, but it still has many supporters in

American law enforcement. Even if the machine cannot provide proof of deception, they say, it reveals whether certain questions make a suspect uncomfortable, which may mean that the suspect is hiding something. In this way, the test results may point to areas that the detectives should investigate further. Military and intelligence organizations also use polygraph testing, as do some employers. In recent years a few state courts have admitted polygraph evidence, although it is not accepted in federal courts.

Whatever the value of sodium thiopental and the polygraph may be, David Meierhofer performed well on both tests. Pointing to the outstanding test results, Meierhofer's attorney demanded that the investigators end their questioning. The attorney also wanted law enforcement to leave his client alone in the future.

With only slight circumstantial evidence against him, Meierhofer was released. Yet the questioning had given Dunbar and the profilers a chance to observe the suspect and to learn more about the kind of person he was. The profilers believed that Meierhofer considered himself to be more clever than the investigators and was proud of having outwitted them. They also thought that he might like to gloat over his crimes. They suggested that the Jaegers attach a recording device to their telephone in case they received a call from the killer, and they coached the family of the missing child on how to respond to such a call.

Exactly one year after Susan Jaeger's kidnapping, her mother received a call from a man who claimed to have Susan with him in Europe. Instead of begging or crying, Mrs. Jaeger remained calm. The caller hung up. The FBI was unable to trace the call because it had been made by someone tapping into a phone line—a skill Meierhofer had learned in Vietnam. Profiler Pat Mullany felt that Meierhofer might crumble if confronted by a strong woman, so Susan's mother went to Montana to meet with him at his lawyer's office. He remained calm during the meeting, but soon afterward Mrs. Jaeger received another call. The caller identified himself as "Mr. Travis," but when Mrs. Jaeger said, "Well, hello, David," he hung up.

The recorded calls did not prove Meierhofer's guilt, but they persuaded a judge to issue a search warrant for Meierhofer's home. There investigators found the remains of both Susan Jaeger and Meierhofer's former girlfriend. Meierhofer was taken to jail, where he made a full confession and then, alone in his cell, hanged himself. The murderer had beaten sodium thiopental and the polygraph, but a psychological profile had pointed the way to solving the two cases.

BRAIN FINGERPRINTING

FORENSIC SCIENTISTS ARE examining a powerful new tool that may let them peer inside a subject's mind. Its inventor, a researcher named Lawrence Farwell, calls his technique brain fingerprinting. Unlike a print made by someone's finger, however, the "brain fingerprint" is not a way of identifying individuals. It measures the brain's reactions to words or images.

When a person sees something that is meaningful to him, something he recognizes, an electrical response that scientists call the P300 wave takes place in his brain. The subject of a brain fingerprinting test wears sensors on the outside of the head and looks at a computer screen that shows a series of words or images. If a P300 wave occurs in the subject's brain, the sensors record it. The idea behind brain fingerprinting is that any word or image that triggers the P300 response must be familiar and significant to the subject.

Brain fingerprinting has great potential in detecting and treating Alzheimer's disease. Forgetfulness is a major symptom of the disease, and brain fingerprinting can show how well a patient's brain is retaining information, and whether medications are helping. The media have focused, though, on brain fingerprinting as a tool for investigating crime. Farwell believes it will be especially useful for clearing suspects. If a suspect fails to have a P300 response to pictures of the crime scene or murder

• • • • •

weapon—carefully chosen images that would be recognized only by the criminal, or by someone who was present when the crime was committed—then the suspect must be innocent.

Critics of brain fingerprinting argue that the technology is not yet proven. Memories change over time, and psychological research shows that people can be confused or mistaken about memories. The scientific community has not yet accepted the P300 response as a reliable sign of memory in all cases. Critics are also concerned that an innocent person who simply read a newspaper article about a crime, or saw television coverage of it, might have a P300 response to an image connected with the crime. Some people have expressed concern that brain fingerprinting could target people who fantasize or think about crimes but have not committed them. This possibility raises serious questions about fairness.

Farwell performed the test on a death row convict named Jimmie Ray Slaughter, convicted in Oklahoma of murdering his girlfriend and their infant daughter. The test, Farwell said, showed that Slaughter was innocent, but the Oklahoma Supreme Court did not admit the test as evidence. The court's position was that brain fingerprinting does not have enough scientific documentation. The state court and the U.S. Supreme Court rejected Slaughter's requests for an appeal. He was executed in 2005.

Scientists, doctors, lawyers, and law enforcement officials are debating the merits and shortcomings of brain fingerprinting. Only time will tell whether this new technology will win enough scientific support to be widely accepted as a forensic tool.

▶ THE BLACK WIDOW OF COBB COUNTY

In the early days of forensic science, poisoners usually killed their victims with what are now called the "classic" poisons: arsenic, cyanide, and strychnine. These days, however, poisoners are much more likely to use medical drugs, such as sleeping pills in overdose amounts, or ordinary household substances that are toxic to humans. Such poisonings may be difficult to detect unless the **medical examiner (ME)** knows what to look for.

In early 1995 Glenn Turner, a police officer in Cobb County, Georgia, showed up at a hospital emergency room with stomach pain and other symptoms that seemed like signs of a severe case of flu. The hospital treated him and released him. Turner died the following day. His body was examined by Dr. Brian Frist, who was a medical examiner—a physician who conducts autopsies in cases of sudden deaths, or deaths from unknown causes. Frist decided that Turner's death was due to a natural cause: problems brought about by an enlarged heart. Julia Lynn Turner, who had married Turner two years earlier, collected more than $150,000 from his life insurance and retirement accounts.

Almost immediately, the widow rented an apartment for herself and a sheriff's deputy named Randy Thompson. Turner had begun a relationship with

Thompson before her husband's death, and now it came into the open. The two then had a child together, and Thompson named Turner as the beneficiary of his insurance. They did not marry, however, and eventually Thompson moved out, although he continued to see Turner. In 2001, after having dinner with Turner, he went to the hospital emergency room, vomiting and complaining of stomach pain. After Thompson was released from the hospital, Turner offered him some comfort food: lime Jell-O. Thompson died the next day. His death was blamed on an irregular heartbeat. His beneficiary, Turner, received about $36,000 in death benefits.

Two young men, both struck down suddenly— was Julia Lynn Turner tragically unlucky in love? Or was there a sinister motive at work? Newspaper accounts of Randy Thompson's death disturbed Glenn Turner's mother. She knew that Julia Lynn Turner was in debt and needed money, and the similarity between the two deaths bothered her. She contacted Thompson's mother. The two women feared that their sons had fallen prey to what is sometimes called a "black widow"—a woman who kills one man after another, usually for profit (the term comes from the black widow spider, a species in which the female sometimes kills and eats the male after they mate).

The two mothers took their suspicions to Dr. Mark Koponen, the deputy chief medical examiner of Georgia's state bureau of investigation. Koponen studied the autopsy reports on both men and noticed that Thompson's kidneys had contained a lot of calcium oxylate crystals, a sign that the kidneys, which absorb harmful substances in the body, had been under some unusual stress. He ordered toxicological tests on samples of Randy Thompson's blood and urine. These samples had been kept after the autopsy, which is standard forensic practice.

Toxicology is the study of foreign substances in the body. The substances may be drugs, poisons, medicines, or other chemicals, all of which affect the body in different ways. Toxicology has two main uses in forensics. Law enforcement officials rely on toxicologists to test substances that may be illegal drugs. Their tests can reveal not just what a drug is, but exactly what materials it contains, which is often a clue to who made it or where it came from. The other main forensic use of toxicology is testing human tissue samples, such as blood, hair, urine, or muscle, to see if they contain drugs or toxins, substances that cause illness or death.

Repeated toxicological testing revealed that before Randy Thompson died, he had somehow consumed ethylene glycol. This toxic chemical compound causes

CATCHING KILLERS WITH SCIENCE | 53

headaches and nausea, followed by death from kidney failure or a heart attack. It is never naturally found in the human body, but it is the main ingredient in antifreeze, the substance added to the water in car radiators to prevent freezing. The cause of Thompson's death was changed to antifreeze poisoning. The reason for the second death was now known. What about the first?

Dr. Brian Frist, the medical examiner who had signed the death certificate for Glenn Turner, arranged to have Turner's body exhumed, or dug up, so that the remains could be tested. Toxicological testing showed the presence of ethylene glycol, so Turner's cause of death was changed, too. Julia Lynn Turner was charged with the murder of her husband. Because the two cases were handled separately, she would later be charged with the murder of Randy Thompson.

During Turner's first trial, her attorneys argued that the presence of ethylene glycol in Glenn Turner's remains could have been due to the embalming fluid used to prepare his body for burial. That defense fell apart when the prosecutors proved that there was no ethylene glycol in the embalming fluid used in *either* burial.

The most important expert witnesses at the trial were the medical examiners and forensic toxicologists who had examined and reexamined the remains of the two dead men. They explained how it had been possible

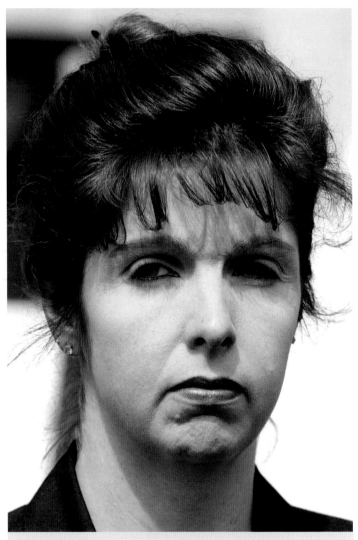

▲ Like many killers, Julia Lynn Turner used the same method of murder on both her victims. The sudden deaths of her husband and lover raised suspicions, leading to the discovery that the two men had been poisoned.

for both deaths to be blamed on natural causes connected with heart trouble, and how forensic screening had brought the true cause of death to light. Frist also described experiments he had conducted with antifreeze. He had found that it could be concealed in certain foods, such as lime Jell-O, that would look and taste completely normal to the victim.

In early 2004 Julia Lynn Turner was convicted of murdering Glenn Turner. Three years later she was convicted of murdering Randy Thompson. She is serving a life sentence in prison.

A key element in the Turner case was the suspicion of Glenn Turner's mother that something just wasn't right about the deaths of two young men, one of them her son. She had no proof, but by calling the authorities' attention to the unexplained similarities, she had gotten them to take a second look at the files, and that had triggered the toxicological tests. The Turner case proves that even the most advanced forensic science may depend, in part, on human intuition.

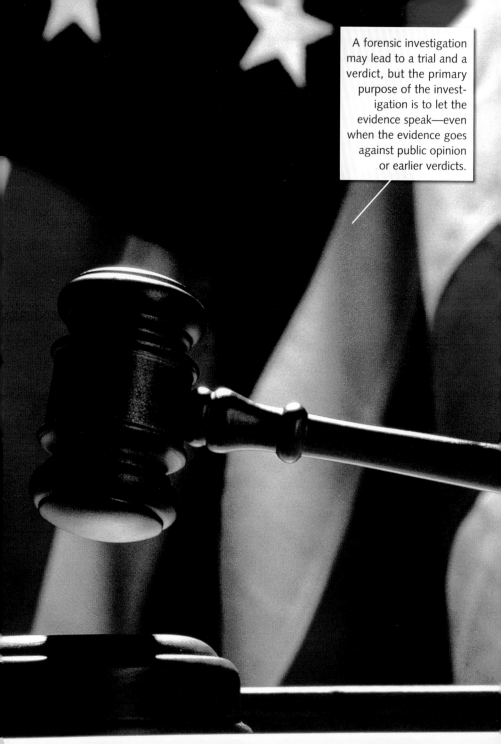

A forensic investigation may lead to a trial and a verdict, but the primary purpose of the investigation is to let the evidence speak—even when the evidence goes against public opinion or earlier verdicts.

CHAPTER THREE

JUSTICE IS SERVED

▼ THE MEN AND WOMEN WHO INVESTIGATE

crimes know that their first duty is to help anyone who is in danger. Beyond that, they have a driving goal: to seek the truth. Forensic science often provides their best chance—perhaps their only chance—of finding it.

The answers to investigators' questions about a case do not always come at once. There may be false starts and delays. Sometimes it takes a long time to unravel the tangled tale of the evidence. But whether they are correcting a mistake, righting a wrong, or proving an accused person's innocence, forensic investigators want to know what really happened, so that justice can be done.

▶ "THE DINGO'S GOT MY BABY!"

Forensic science is not always perfect. One example of forensics gone wrong unfolded in Australia in the 1980s. To Australians, the Lindy Chamberlain case was the crime of the twentieth century. To forensic scientists, law enforcement officers, and prosecutors everywhere, it stands as a grim reminder that investigations must be more than thorough. They must be impartial.

The tragedy began at the foot of Uluru, also called Ayers Rock. This huge outcropping of red stone in the heart of the Australian outback attracts tourists from all over Australia and the world. In 1980 Lindy and Michael Chamberlain and their three young children traveled from their home in Mount Isa, a mining town in northeastern Australia, to explore Uluru. After a day of sightseeing, they joined the crowd of people who had pitched tents at a local campground. Two of the Chamberlains' children slept in the tent, while Michael and Lindy cooked their dinner at a barbecue grill not far away.

Suddenly, Michael Chamberlain heard a cry from the tent. As Lindy ran toward the sound, she saw a dingo, one of the wild dogs of Australia, backing out through the open tent flaps. It disappeared into the darkness. Lindy looked into the tent and saw that her youngest child, nine-week-old Azaria, was missing. Blood was

▲ In 1980 a baby disappeared near this Australian landmark. Was her disappearance a tragic accident or a violent murder? Forensic investigators clashed over the question.

spattered where the little girl had been lying. Lindy ran from the tent, screaming, "The dingo's got my baby!"

Park rangers and others searched through the night. They found dingo prints near the Chamberlains' tent, and other tourists reported seeing dingoes nearby, but there was no trace of Azaria. The next few days brought no good news, and the Chamberlains returned home. Eight days after Azaria's disappearance, some of the baby's clothes were found, torn and blood-stained, near a dingo den.

▶ FORENSICS GONE WRONG

Because Azaria's disappearance had been viewed as an accident, not a crime, the scene was badly mishandled from a forensic point of view. Rushing feet trampled the dingo prints. No one photographed the tent until hours had passed. Worse still, television news programs showed police officers holding the baby's clothes in bare hands, moving them this way and that to show the bloodstains. The garments should have been sealed immediately for forensic examination.

By this time, police in Australia's Northern Territory, where Uluru is located, had become suspicious of the Chamberlains. They believed that Azaria's death was no accident, and they were not alone. Led by the media, which whipped up frenzied interest in the story, many Australians turned against the Chamberlains. To some, the idea that a dingo would take a baby was absurd. No one had ever heard of such a thing. Could a dingo, an animal about the size of a coyote and smaller than the average German shepherd dog, carry a 10-pound baby? And what about the jacket that Lindy Chamberlain claimed Azaria had been wearing? Why wasn't it found with the rest of the clothes?

One strike against the Chamberlains was their religion. They belonged to the Seventh-Day Adventist Church, which some Australians viewed with prejudice stemming from ignorance and suspicion. There were even ridiculous rumors that Azaria had been killed in a satanic ritual. Another strike was Lindy's behavior. Private and self-possessed, she did not fit people's image of the proper grief-stricken mother. Many articles described her as "dry-eyed," making the fact that she did not sob in public seem like a sign of guilt.

An official hearing into Azaria's disappearance was held in late 1980. Dr. Kenneth Brown, a forensic odontologist (specialist in teeth and tooth marks), testified

▲ One dispute in the Chamberlain case revolved around the dingo, an animal that was not previously known to attack humans.

that the cuts in Azaria's clothing appeared to have been made by scissors or a knife, not by dingo teeth. The official in charge of the hearing was a coroner, or medical examiner. After pointing out that the Chamberlains had suffered "months of innuendo, suspicion, and probably the most malicious gossip ever witnessed in this country," the coroner ruled that Azaria's death was accidental, and that a wild dingo, not any member of her family, was responsible. The mismanagement of the evidence had been blindingly clear to the coroner.

Neither Dr. Brown nor the Northern Territory law enforcement agencies, however, was satisfied with the coroner's verdict. With the help of several well-known forensic scientists, they pulled together enough supposed evidence against the Chamberlains to get the state to hold a second hearing on Azaria's disappearance. Several experts testified that they had not been able to duplicate the tears in Azaria's clothing using similar clothing, a dingo tooth, a dingo skull, and even a pack of dingoes in a zoo. Their conclusion was that the clothing had been cut, not bitten. Dogs' teeth, these experts agreed, could not cut through cloth, only tear it.

James Cameron, a famous pathologist from London, claimed that one of the stains on Azaria's clothing was a bloody handprint, even though neither the Chamberlains' lawyer nor the coroner could see anything resembling a handprint. Cameron's testimony led people to think that Azaria's throat had been cut, or possibly that the baby had been decapitated.

A forensic biologist named Joy Kuhl provided the most damaging testimony. She claimed to have found microscopic traces of human blood all over the interior of the Chamberlains' car, on a pair of nail scissors in the car, and on the zipper of Michael Chamberlain's camera bag. Earlier examinations had missed the blood because the car had been cleaned. Kuhl had found the stains by treating materials from the car with orthotolidine, a chemical that turns bright blue in the presence of even tiny amounts of blood.

Faced with so many experts eager to provide testimony, the coroner called for a trial. Lindy Chamberlain was charged with the murder of Azaria. Michael Chamberlain, thought to have helped his wife cover up the killing, was charged as an accessory.

▶ FORENSICS GONE RIGHT

The trial was a replay of the second hearing. The same experts presented the same evidence. Joy Kuhl, presenter of the blood evidence, had an awkward moment when she was forced to explain that the original test materials that had seemingly revealed blood in the Chamberlains' car had been destroyed. Although she claimed that was standard lab procedure, the vast majority of criminal forensics professionals would disagree. Great efforts are made to preserve all evidence, including testing materials, for possible use in any future trials or forensic examinations.

The Chamberlains' defense lawyer had found forensic experts to support the Chamberlains. One of them testified that Kuhl was incompetent and that her test results were unreliable. Another questioned Cameron's finding of the "bloody handprint." The defense also argued that no one had put forward any reason why Lindy Chamberlain might have killed her little girl, or any evidence of mental disorder. Still, the forensic evidence against the Chamberlains seemed overwhelming. The jury found them guilty in October 1982. Lindy went to prison for life. Michael received a suspended sentence.

The Chamberlain case might have ended there, except for a group of people, including some scientists, who believed that Lindy Chamberlain had been unjustly convicted. They thought that the law enforcement community of the Northern Territory was so determined to find Chamberlain guilty, and so unwilling to admit that it might be wrong, that it had accepted without question any results or opinions that supported her guilt.

▲ Michael and Lindy Chamberlain leave court in 1982. The court had just determined that the two would be tried for the murder of their daughter.

One member of the group carried out tests with his own dog, Susie. He discovered that she sometimes tore cloth and sometimes cut right through it with her teeth. When he was finally allowed to see Azaria's clothing, it looked just like the cloth that Susie had bitten. Another expert determined that hairs found on the clothing had come from a dingo.

The strongest blow against the Chamberlains had been Kuhl's testimony about their supposedly blood-drenched car and possessions. When the investigators looked more closely, however, they found that what Kuhl had identified as a "spray" of blood was actually a spray-on soundproofing material used in automobile manufacturing. Other cars of the same model had the same pattern.

What about the other bloodstains? A search of the scientific literature on orthotolidine revealed that the chemical reacts with substances other than blood. One of those substances is copper, which had long been mined at Mount Isa, the Chamberlains' home. Smoke from the mines hung over the town much of the time. A simple test showed that orthotolidine reacted with the dust found on dozens of ordinary objects in Mount Isa. Kuhl's blood evidence was thoroughly undermined.

Fate lent a hand in early 1986, when a visitor to Uluru found Azaria's missing jacket, partly buried in sand, near where the other clothes had been found. By itself, the garment proved only that Lindy had told the truth about what Azaria was wearing. Together with the new forensic evidence that questioned the original evidence, however, the little jacket was enough to get Lindy released from prison.

A Royal Commission of Inquiry was called to review the case. Its report, released in 1988, was deeply critical of the shoddy work by park rangers, police, the Northern Territory prosecutors, and certain forensic scientists whose evidence had been far weaker than their claims for it. According to the commission, the case never should have gone to trial.

Eventually Lindy Chamberlain received a cash settlement from the Australian government for her wrongful imprisonment. Many Australians, however, continued to consider her guilty. Some people said that even though the original forensic evidence against Chamberlain had been discredited, that did not prove that a dingo really did take her baby. Recent events, however, have cast new light on Lindy Chamberlain's story about that tragic night in 1980.

A couple from Queensland was camping on Fraser Island off the eastern coast of Australia in 1998 when a dingo seized their thirteen-month-old child—much larger and heavier than Azaria Chamberlain had been. The animal began dragging the toddler away, but when the child's father ran at the dingo, it released its prey and fled. In 2001, on the same island, dingoes attacked two brothers, ages seven and nine, killing the older boy. No one now doubts that a dingo can, and will, carry off a baby.

▶ ACCIDENT OR MURDER?

Forensic fumbles like that in the Chamberlain case are rare, but they do occur. Good forensic science, however, has been the key to freeing many innocent people who were wrongly convicted of crimes. Clayton Johnson is just one of thousands of people who have reason to be grateful to forensics.

In 1989 Johnson was a schoolteacher. He and his wife, Janice, lived with their children in the Canadian village of Shelburne, on the island of Nova Scotia. One morning at 7:40 A.M. Clare Thompson, the Johnsons' neighbor across the street, spoke to Janice on the telephone. She heard Janice say goodbye to her husband as he left for school. The two women chatted until 7:50 A.M. Moments later, a friend arrived at the Johnson house and found Janice lying unconscious at the bottom of the basement stairs, bleeding from the head. The friend called for an ambulance at 7:54 A.M. Janice Johnson died later that day without regaining consciousness.

The fall had been a terrible accident. Two of the Johnsons' neighbors volunteered to clean up the basement, which had not been photographed. They reported to the accident investigators that there had been a lot of blood on the wall near the third step, but only a little on the floor.

The coroner, Dr. Roland Perry, decided that Janice had tripped and fallen headfirst down the stairs. On the way down she caught her head in a gap between the stairs and the wall. At that time her head was wounded and bled on the wall.

The community was sympathetic to the widowed Clayton Johnson—until he began dating a younger woman. People criticized him for this, and soon a rumor made the rounds: two months before Janice died, Johnson had taken out a life insurance policy in her name. Suddenly the accident looked suspicious. The helpful neighbors who had washed the bloodstains from the basement changed their story. Now they said that blood had been everywhere on the floor and walls.

The police passed the revised description of the scene to two pathologists, who decided that the case now looked like murder, not an accidental fall. They believed that Janice Johnson had been standing at the bottom of the stairs when someone clubbed her, probably with a board, causing her to bleed on the wall as she fell. The obvious suspect was her husband. The insurance money from Janice's death would have been useful to Clayton Johnson, who was in debt.

What about Clare Thompson's testimony that she had been talking on the phone to Janice Johnson until 7:50 A.M.? If that were true, Clayton Johnson would have had just four minutes to return to the house, batter his wife (without getting any blood on himself), dispose of the weapon (which was never found), and leave before the friend arrived. This seemed impossible, so prosecutors decided that Clare Thompson must be mistaken about the time of her phone conversation with Janice. The call must have ended at 7:40 A.M. That would have given Johnson enough time to bludgeon Janice and make his getaway.

The case against Johnson was desperately weak, but feelings against him ran high because of what people regarded as his misbehavior with the younger woman, whom he had by then married. When Johnson went to trial for murder in 1993, the jury found him guilty. He received a life sentence.

▶ RIGHTING A WRONG

Throughout the ordeal Johnson had insisted he was innocent, and he continued to do so from prison. Eventually the case came to the attention of the Association in Defence of the Wrongly Convicted. This Canadian organization is one of a number of groups around the world that are dedicated to correcting miscarriages of justice. Drawing on the skills of lawyers and forensic scientists, many of whom provide their services at no charge, these men and women

▲ Clayton Johnson, convicted of murdering his wife, hugs his daughters at the start of his appeal—a second trial that would challenge the findings of the first.

investigate cases in which an innocent person may have been wrongfully convicted. The Canadian organization decided to take on Johnson's case.

As soon as a new set of investigators took a close look at the evidence, the case against Johnson crumbled. The life insurance policy, for example, turned out to be less

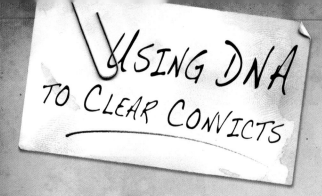

IN 1982 JERRY MILLER was convicted of kidnapping, robbing, and raping a woman in a Chicago parking garage. He served twenty-four years in prison. After being released in 2006, he was required to register as a sex offender and to wear an ankle bracelet so that authorities could track his movements.

Miller had been convicted because two attendants at the parking garage had identified him as the attacker. The victim thought he was the attacker, but she wasn't sure. For twenty-five years, however, Miller claimed he was innocent. In April of 2007, a DNA test was performed on biological material left by the rapist on the victim's clothing. The results clearly showed that Miller had been telling the truth. He was not guilty.

Miller was the two-hundredth convicted person in the United States to be exonerated, or proven innocent, by DNA testing. "The first 200 DNA exonerations have transformed the criminal justice system in this country," says Barry Scheck. He and fellow attorney Peter Neufeld founded the Innocence Project at the Benjamin N. Cardozo School of Law at Yeshiva University in 1992. Since then they have worked to make DNA testing available to prison inmates who might be cleared by this miracle of modern forensic science. The Innocence

The justice system makes mistakes, but sometimes forensic science can correct them. Jerry Miller, convicted and imprisoned for rape, was later proven innocent by DNA testing.

Project has also analyzed the 200 exonerations, with the goal of identifying the factors that contribute to wrongful convictions. According to its research, the chief reasons for wrongful convictions are eyewitness misidentification, forensic errors, racism, and false confessions. The efforts of the Innocence Project and other concerned people and groups have led forty states to pass laws giving convicted criminals the right to DNA tests that might prove their innocence. Other states are considering similar laws.

suspicious than it had first appeared. The school where Johnson worked had offered insurance to all of its employees at the same time, and 40 percent of them, including Johnson, had taken advantage of the offer.

A pathologist who reviewed the case suggested that Janice Johnson had fallen down the stairs backward, and by accident. Herbert McDowell, director of a New York State forensic laboratory and an expert in interpreting blood spatter patterns, came up with a way to test this theory. McDowell constructed an exact duplicate of the basement stairway in the Johnson house. He marked the wall and the third step with blue chalk where the neighbors had *first* said they found blood.

Then McDowell found a model who was exactly Janice Johnson's height and weight. He provided her with a helmet, attached her to a safety harness, and flipped her backward from the top step. As she went down, her head struck the wall and the step, right on the chalk marks. When she landed at the bottom, there were blue chalk marks on her helmet. They corresponded to Janice Johnson's head wound.

Under pressure to give Clayton Johnson a second trial, the state reopened the case. When the prosecution declared that it had no evidence against Johnson, he was freed after more than five years in prison. By taking the trouble to build a duplicate stairway and to test the fall with a model, McDowell had used the forensic technique of crime scene reconstruction. In Johnson's case, however, the reconstruction showed that what had happened on the scene was not a crime but an accident. Forensics, so often used to prove guilt, can also prove innocence.

NO DUMPING

PENALTIES INCLUDE:

1. Up to a $10,000 FINE
(La. State Senate Bill No. 963)

2. Possible Vehicle Seizure
(New Orleans City Ordinance
No. 24412 20000861)

3. Up to 6 months imprisonment
(La. State Senate Bill No. 972)

New Orleans Business & Industrial District

For questions regarding legal trash disposal, call the City of
New Orleans Department of Sanitation at (504) 299-3670.

Trash piles up behind a
"No Dumping" sign in
Lousiana. Illegal dump-
ing of trash or toxic
wastes is one of the
most common forms of
environmental crime.

CHAPTER FOUR

MORE THAN
MURDER

▼ HOMICIDE IS NOT THE ONLY CRIME

solved with forensic science. Investigators have called on forensic experts for help in all kinds of cases. In 2004, for example, British police captured a man who had been robbing the elderly. One victim had managed to pull off the robber's mask, which had the robber's DNA on it. When police ran a profile of the DNA from the mask through their database, they found a very similar sample from a man who had once been convicted of possessing marijuana. The one-time drug offender was arrested for robbery.

Drug cases demand the help of forensic experts in chemistry and toxicology. These professionals analyze samples taken in evidence and determine if they are illegal substances. Chemists and toxicologists also help solve environmental crimes, such as the illegal dumping of toxic wastes. Other forensic experts investigate crimes that are committed over the Internet, or with the help of computers. From identity theft to scams and frauds, cybercrimes are solved by forensic computer scientists who know how to find evidence hidden on hard drives and can follow a chain of Web sites and e-mails that may stretch around the world.

▶ WILDLIFE FORENSICS

Criminalistics meets biology in the fast-growing field of wildlife forensics, the scientific investigation of crimes against wildlife. The most common wildlife crimes are illegal trade and illegal hunting. Illegal trade involves commerce in endangered species or parts of endangered species, such as elephant ivory. Illegal hunting, or poaching, involves killing a protected animal or hunting it outside the legal hunting season.

In 1988 the U.S. Fish and Wildlife Service (USFWS) opened the country's first wildlife forensics laboratory in Ashland, Oregon. The facility was enlarged in 2007. One addition to the lab was a high-tech biological containment area—a place for the safe storage and examination of materials that might be biologically

▲ Rangers at Tsavo National Park, in the African nation of Kenya, examine elephant ivory seized from poachers, or illegal hunters. The trade in ivory and other animal parts threatens the survival of many wildlife species.

hazardous, such as diseased animal carcasses. Another was a "bug room," where beetles devour the flesh of carcasses, leaving clean skeletons for study.

Both U.S. and international law enforcement agencies send materials to the National Fish and Wildlife Forensics Laboratory to be analyzed. Among other things, the lab has pioneered techniques for using microscopes to examine the grain lines in ivory. These

ILLEGAL LUXURIES

THE NATIONAL FISH and Wildlife Forensics Laboratory in Ashland, Oregon, has provided crucial evidence in criminal cases involving caviar (fish eggs that are prized as a luxury food) and rhinoceros horn, which some people mistakenly believe to have medicinal properties. Several Russian smugglers received convictions and fines in 2002, after DNA testing at the lab proved that caviar imported into the United States came from the Caspian Sea sturgeon, a protected species. In 2007, after scientists at the lab performed genetic tests on a so-called herbal medicine, a shop owner in Portland, Oregon, pleaded guilty to violating the Endangered Species Act. He had sold potions illegally made with the horn of the black rhinoceros, one of the most endangered species in the world.

. . . . .